The Thursday Poets' Anthology

Dreams and Realities

Important Notices

Library of Congress LCCN: 2022918073

ISBN-13: 979-8986360300

Compiled by elliot m rubin. Edited by elliot m rubin and Rodney Richards. Some poems previously copyrighted by their authors.

Cover designed and created by Jesse Richards

Photos chosen and owned or licensed for commercial use from Shutterstock or others by respective authors, or in the public domain

Published by ABLiA Media LLC, Hamilton New Jersey, USA

First edition

Disclaimer

Table of Contents

Introduction

About three years ago, Elliot Rubin brought a group of poets together, originally on Friday mornings, to share, read, listen, and offer critiques of the poetry we each wrote. This later became Thursdays, with some folks leaving, others joining. As Zoom host and moderator, Elliot keeps the group moving, learning, and improving. The atmosphere is collegial, often funny, never adversarial.

Critique improves the writing and supports and encourages the writer or poet, who can accept, change, or reject any observations or suggestions.

In poetry, critique involves finding the theme of the piece, its flow and rhythm, sounds and impact, metaphors, and double meanings. Good critique is more than pointing out syntactical, spelling, and punctuation errors, although it includes those.

Besides offering suggestions, making observations, and sharing impressions it means feeling and seeing form and images carefully painted by precise vocabularies, even spaces. It means seeking brevity and clarity within the poet's purpose. It seeks to find the poet's connections with the reader's or listener's spirit, mind, heart, and soul.

Poetry transports one through the world and into the universe on a path of discovery to dreams and realities not experienced or expressed before.

This compilation highlights ninety-one poems we selected to share for this book, poems that have tangible and intangible meanings to us and, we hope, to you.

Poets and their poems follow

Carol Johns

Autumn Days

My name is Autumn, nurturing, mature, abundant.
Heavy-hipped, I languish my days reclining
in riots of red, yellow, orange hues,
palpable against clear, crisp air.
Voluptuous, confident, my beauty richer
than my humid Summer sister
or my greenstick daughter, whose
emergent elegance is fleeting, tenuous.
Survey my bounty:
rich, red tomatoes, plump pumpkins,
succulent squash, shapely, womanly.
Fall into my spell,
Breathe in the smoldering fire of leaves,
feel your pulse quicken
with the harmony of nature.
For mine is the very witching time of life
when Earth stirs humans and animals alike
to nest, brew, feast, and luxuriate
in harvest celebration.
I wait in readiness, unafraid
of the advancing Ice Queen.

By the Numbers

Wire probes to
know the truth
of my clinical heart.
Bleeps, graph lines,
and pressure counts
to define an
identity so trivial.
I plead for recognition,
banter, laugh, charm,
but technicians turn away
to gather facts,
record the concrete knowable.
        Where to gauge
the essence, the spirit
of my warm blood,
        how to measure
the quickened cells, the hunger
of its beat,
        who to call my
heart by its human name?

Earthbound

Brace of night air against warm lungs,
my mortal vision draws up to the matrix of heaven.
The clear stars stir my spirit
as I reach to see the edge of time.
My eyes search deep infinity to find your homestar
where I will meet you someday.
Then I will speak
 all the tenderness I did not say,
if you will still listen.
But for now
the giant hills, coursing rivers,
sweet-grass meadows,
heavy green waters of the ocean
will be the boundaries of my world.
I study the smooth stones of my walkway
as I close the garden gate.

Noble Half-Truths

You have taught, oh Buddha
that suffering will cease
when we have rid ourselves of desire,
that the doorway to the Secret Essences
will open to us if
we walk the Middle Way.
So I have
turned from passion and appetite,
loved, but lay claim to no one,
watched in silence as
the ghosts of my energy
dissolve into nothingness.
But I have not glimpsed
any sacred mysteries,
except to say,
Oh Illustrious One,
that to live without desire
is a kind of suffering too.

Birth Mother

Storm out of Eden, rip the lush ferns from their stems
in righteous anger, this is no paradise for you.
March into an unknown landscape of brown, dry desert,
salt marshes that stink of fish decay,
perhaps gravel pathways to a new valley.
Anything is better than submission to his control.
You are the image of God, not the servant,
but even the scribes wrote
you out of history.
Take heart, you are not fallen
with the players,
you are still immortal like the God who made you.
Travel the earth for the ages
in search of daughters
who know you not
And have no one to call divine mother,
    Lilith.

Shush

Kafka* was full of it:
now I listen hard
for the world to unfold its rhythm.
I've waited and waited
for the sound and tone of small nuances,
but not even a blue note
has sputtered onto the page.
Why face the torture of barren bars
to create emotional music
when all the universe
seems to have exploded
into the crack of machine gun fire?
Language, the beloved melody, shoots
bullets of hate and division.
Sometimes the less noise, the better.

*Somewhere Kafka states that in order to write, one just needs to
sit and listen. The idea will come.

Stay, my one,

place your dreams on the pillow
next to my dreams.
Let's live in the land of touch and moment.
Full lifetimes we have lived with others,
whose blood mingled with our own.
Alone we traveled the long journey
to comprehend that they are gone,
and with them our cells
    now embedded in death.
So, do not go, my one,
stay with me in the realm of touch and feeling,
for we are disappearing things
and nothing else seems to matter.

Show Don't Tell
Inspired by David Maley's *Echo*

You struggle to declare yourself
with three expected words,
the three most exposing syllables.
Feel no pressure to conform
      because you,
            pop open the good umbrella to shelter us
            in a sudden downpour,
            I slip my hand through your arm,
            feel you press it tight against
            your warm side;
      because you
            have a ready embrace when the world
            outside has offended me,
            let me belong in your personal space;
      because you
            emit a certain light from your eyes
            when you see the 17 year old girl
            transposed over this mature face,
            have the good grace to still see beauty.
What vocabulary can say more?
You speak a sweeter language
Sensual, private, wordless,
            And I have heard.

Tribunal

Tribunal Carol Johns

March 16, 2021

Three gaunt men, older than time

sit on the high altar of the office.

Dressed in suit cloth, originally black,

now faded to drabness,

they have aged into the very wood

of the courtroom.

The panels of the walls, planks of the floor,

Gray, minimal, functional.

The air is stagnant, joyless,

Puritan.

Staring down through creased, hooded eyes

that still retain a glimmer,

they observe me, in the dock,

not with particular malice,

but more with curiosity,

as if examining a lower phylum

of the animal kingdom.

Do you repent, they demand.

Of what do I stand charged?

I study the hard floor boards,

my defense futile.

Their scripture, their laws, their justice,

this is the somber world they have created,

not the glory of God.

As I mumble my apology

for being human,

my mind detaches from

the severity of my plight.

My attention is drawn to

a tall paned window in the back of the room

through which sunlight streams in rays,

the dust motes dance playfully in the beams.

Outside, the promise of a paradise

of green, living motion,

the place I belong.

No matter what happens in here,

I know that I am going into His

world of color.

Dona McCormack

A Little Fire

"A little fire is quickly trodden out, which being suffered,
rivers cannot quench." –William Shakespeare, *Henry VIII*

I know smoke
when I smell it

Alarms
ring along
my spine
when I sense
acrid bits
of past life
floating in thin
choking air

Hammers
hit bells
the day
I met you—

I should have
stamped
you right
out

I know smoke
when I smell it

But you linger
like incense
and opium—

Until every inch
of my scorched
earth
sprouts
with saplings

Aphorism #2

sometimes
the need
to love
sustains us
more than
the love
we receive

Distilled in Black

Your eyes
have no color
but black
at the pupil,
rippling wells
of inky depth, swirl
with potential
symphonies of your soul
liquid music
from which your wand
twirls out the dance
of your newborn ideas

Black happens
when a surface
drinks in
all the light
Give me the blackest
of your eyes
You—the most
of you
distilled
in black

Easy Catch

Banana spider spins
his web in a corner
full of Florida crosswind,
and the flies blow
out of control
right into his stomach.

He catches
leaves
plastic bags
tiny fuel receipts
candy wrappers

He doesn't catch
all the litter
that rips right through
taut threads

He rebuilds nightly
Eats rarely
Moves on quickly

Sepia

depression is the laziest fruit
makes me ravenous

meaning colors
what is a mirror,
otherwise a sepia movie in 8MM.
meaning is convex,
depression caves in.

blueberries black
as birds, as earth,
depression
has no depth.

Give Me Black
Give Me Black

feeling blue is better than
the tug of this gravity

Epitaphs

I write about how
in love we were
back in our best days

I use pencil
so tears
won't wash words away

I mean the poems
to be epitaphs
burnable ones

when it isn't enough
anymore
to say

You're dead to me

I Am the Poem

I felt it first
when you touched
the pencil,
stroked your fingers
along the smooth barrel—
Applied soft pressure
with your fingertips
Let the pencil settle
into its sharpened
gray point

Word by word, you write
me closer
leg, you write
then, *thigh*
  —*breath*

You fill me
into the page
make
so many marks—
all at once, I am upon you

I waited
in your pencil tip—
whispered against me,
full on the page,
where I
moaned your name

Lilacs

I miss lilacs
can almost smell
blossoms
on the crack
cold wind
Legs lift
just high enough
to work steps forward
    Thick flakes
    imitate snowballs
    tumble eternally, loosely
    collect, build, accumulate
Shovel scrapes at them
I remember your determined blade
We're digging a path to Spring, Evelyn
Let's go.

Gasping breath
detects frozen metal
Lungs ring
    like tears coming

I miss lilacs
I start to dig your path

| Dona McCormack

Right in the Kisser

He kissed his knuckles
in the sweaty sun
opened his eyes
to see her smile
at him
from her driver's window
mysterious
beautiful woman

she swung her wheel
like a weapon
blew out his brain
with a shot of exhaust
turned the corner
out of view

His stomach inflated
floated up his throat
His heart twirled—
a punch to his soul

Like being
electrocuted
Like being
in love

elliot m rubin

forever in love

with her body
wrapped in his arms
dreams come true
problem is for how long

this gorgeous woman
is everything he wants
life could not be better,
except she won't be there long

soon his hour will be up
she will again become
a dream of desire
as his date leaves
for her next appointment

an old man in hospice

as dusk fast approaches
his once fruitful vine,
now withered and bare,
knows the future
as the mighty gardener
      waits
to prune his orchard
until nothing's left
but a dead semblance
of a virile organ
while beautiful young butterflies
which once suckled its succor
now fly past
to alight on young, vibrant vines
to seek nourishment
and propagate
while he lies silently still,
and watches

difference

when i was

        20 and she 70
        i thought her very old

        30 and she 70
        i thought her very elderly

      40 and she 70
      she now looks more mature than old

      50 and she 70
      she begins to look much better to me

      60 and she 70
      wow is she attractive

      70 and she 70
      boy is she is hot
                but what can i do now?

nameless dancer

at eight tonight
she walks in the stage door
and opens her locker to change–
     six-inch silver heels,
     a matching, tiny g-string
     and see-through bra
     are her costume–
she gives the dee-jay her music
then sits, drinks a cup of caffeine-laced coffee,
and waits for her time on stage–
some say she is a victim
used by men for prurient urges,
truth is
she thinks they are the victim
as she plays to their weakness
and goes home
in early morning hours
with pockets full
     of undeclared cash
     earned with every bump
     and lap-grind dance

freedom

she knows she is free
slavery is illegal
yet there are frustrations
her marriage was arranged
her husband pays all bills
her children came one after the other
her husband allows her selected friends
he tells her what is for dinner,
then she cooks
she knows she is free
slavery is illegal
yet she feels enslaved

indispensable

what would men do
  without them
who will be there
  to correct them
oh, the mess they could make
  by themselves
good thing
  the best thing
they ever did
  was find someone
who has the patience
  of a saint
and the fortitude
  to be a wife

the last hearse

it was number seventeen
if anyone counted through tears
this week the last child was buried
with its flowers and stuffed toys

included in the tiny coffin
are a handful of lead bullets
scattered throughout its organs
along with a parent's heartbreak

missing from all the week's funerals
are the laws to prevent this again
seems guns have more rights than kids
immediately afterward   the hearse refuels

loan shark

she was a cold-hearted bitch
never shed a tear or even blinked
if they didn't pay back a loan
she took their home or brand, new car

her step-father drank and beat her
her next-door neighbor raped her
her husband cheated on her
then ran away, cleaned out their cash

banks wouldn't hire her
but the local loan shark did
she led collections every day
when you saw her, you did pay

cars eventually wear out
many factors can cause crashes
she had one too many collections
when her wheels came spinning off

she didn't know what hit her
maybe the little girl whose dad beat her
brought back memories of youth-
she had him disappear, then

took her savings, the young girl, and
headed out to start over
no plans of where to land
no plans of what to do

grief

he stood at the edge
of a sheer cliff for minutes
closed his eyes, and waited

then jumped, he knew
it would be a painless death
and would be instant

the torment of life
since his only child was killed
in a school shooting

was too much to bear,
it broke his will to live on
he wanted to die

life cycle

the angel of death
walks through many fields
as the farmer watches,
curious,
as to which individual crop
will be harvested

there are so many
varieties
to choose from
yet death
is not deterred

with a steady gait
it walks forward
    selections are
    indiscriminate
newly planted
as well as ripe
    it doesn't matter

eventually

all get picked–
while the farmer
ignores sorrows
and continues
to seed the fields

Jill Sharon Kimmelman

Dancing In The Kitchen

Original wedding portrait of
poet's grandparents,
June 1939

Sixty years, together still
they dance in the kitchen like movie stars
from 1939

With her eyes closed
she imagines herself to be this man's siren
all heady scents, fiery hair, throaty whispers

She could be a star of the silver screen
alabaster wrists, swan neck
flashing emeralds and rubies
the whisper of her caresses
delivered by hands in long satin gloves

With his eyes shut, he could be the UPS man
twenty-five years old in summer shorts
flashing a devil of a smile
His lips deliver a commanding brush of
sea-deep kisses

rocking her from her toes to her cerebellum
and back again

There is music, a solo saxophone
drifting in through the open windows
soul-stirring on a cool and scented breeze

Icy cocktails are produced
as smooth as slipping skin, he removes her gloves
allowing her fingers to graze the rim of
her frosted glass, pluck a briny glistening olive
place it between his teeth

It's a shabby room
scuffed up floors, a patched screen door
counter-tops in avocado green

He washes, she dries
that's the way it's always been
sweet tea and ice-cold beer
to toast another perfect sunset

As if he had arranged it all just for her pleasure
his face crinkles with that funny
lopsided smile she knows so well

He fiddles with an old black radio
slow sweet jazz fills the kitchen
spilling into every corner
crossing the room, he takes her hand

Sixty years of Saturday nights
still dancing in the kitchen.

Spring 2012, from *You are the Poem* poetry collection

A Letter To My Daughters

In a large house with hidden closets aplenty
you, my precious children once played
I watched you turn yourselves invisible
cracked apart your little fingers to peek
during a jolly round of hide and seek

In closets like our's
mingled cedar with dainty perfumes
you were Hansel and Gretel
hiding for imaginary reasons
behind each door stood boxes atop boxes
shoes tagged for each outfit
jewelry, color, heel height & seasons

You never knew how close you came
to all I secured in great secrecy with care
excitement, nostalgia, perhaps a bright tear
a passionate celebration of what you would find
all of it simply awaiting you there

Two little girls joyous
making games so very merry
seeking refuge from that tall skinny witch
in black shoes, black hose, tall black hat
from a fairytale that promised no good fairies

That is where you shall find them
thousands upon thousands of my words
penned and locked away
my legacy
a bit lofty a name for what they are
nothing more after all
than notes from a mum you can barely recall

Written so long ago
your brother was but a babe at my breast
you girls were my dearest of treasures
young swans dancing, silken braids, matching ribbons
all remembered pleasures
a moment of grace giving thanks for God's best

Each crisp cream linen page
with splashes of Schiaparelli and Renoir
to honor the imagination
that has always soared within

It mattered not a whit if skies
were dark and gray
where pears drooped on branches
heavy with fruit
those violet blossoms crystallized
trapped in amber like butterflies

With each slim volume, before I began to write
I chose a color, a reason, a mood, a season

Spring's must come first!

When that glorious season permeated my being
I reached with both hands for pinks
pencils, charcoal sticks, paints and pens

Pinks
Peonies, lilacs, champagne, blankets, roses,
so very much more
pinks for the daughters
I shall forever adore

Oh I so hope it will turn out
that way for you
brave, brilliant, bold, the palest blush
a palette of pinks in every possible hue

For your very own daughters,
the little girls you named for me
who could imagine such a joy
a thing a heart can almost touch
but still can never see.

Winter 2022 by Jill Sharon Kimmelman

Rapscallion's Toys

I will make you a room inside my house, fill it with your treasures
antique trains, matchbox cars, ancient weathered
long-playing record albums, your maps and photographs

What is this your eyes are telling me, you never had such treasures
nothing ever given meant just for little boys
not a lone memory of scratched and dented
well-loved toys?

Your songs come from the only soundtrack you have ever known
pieces of holiday hymns floating in the air, late night street
sounds, half-forgotten lyrics
these have become your long-cherished talisman

Someone has brought me you, a filled-with-sweetness-man-child
devoid of memories, denied love far too long, desperate for
celebrations only read about in dog-eared scribbled-in
hand-me down books

I will carve for you a place inside my heart
bring you all the treasures from my own childhood
easy bake ovens that turn out perfectly round
petite cakes
dolls with painted china faces and stiff petticoats
games with names like twister and candy land

Now confusion clouds your eyes
cry if you must, cry if it helps
take it in slowly as you begin to learn this foreign thing
called play

Let me fill your soul with all the joy you have
never known

A lifetime is far too long to wait for a childhood
to begin.

First publication, Spring 2022
Social Justice, anthology edited by Lisa Joy Tomey & Zan Johns
Publisher, Prolific Pulse Press, LLC

Get Out Mister!

Today
an ultimatum arrived
delivered by a child in her knock off suit
badge affixed
lofty letters behind her name
She struts towards a nameless patient's room
in red-bottom heels, matching manicured nails
No knock, why bother
she's met him before, that man in bed B
hospital gossip spreads faster than wildfire
she's heard all about his struggles from that
damned disorder. PTSD
From the lips of strangers she has
what she thinks she needs
many have praised him, even more
offer prayers
she is baffled by such devotion
no wish to hear his pleas
Her lips shine like those shoes
as bright as a light atop a miner's hat
He is lost inside a nightmare
inside a fire that lit up his skies
seared skin, broken limbs
five decades later
he still can hear his brother's cries
She slides two pages across a table
to define this man's future
points and taps as if he were blind
she lets her fingers do the talking
this is where you must sign

It takes a certain skill to kill another's will
to steal their dreams
witness one writhing in pain
Years spent in library carrels and lecture halls
to earn those letters behind her name
all wasted..,what a shame
They will never reach her shuttered heart
the click of her heels is all that remains.

Summer 2022 by Jill Sharon Kimmelman

When Barbie Met Ken

There are scribbles on the pages of my date book
chicken-scratch patches, my personal code
intimacy lost and gained

An indelible stamp of your plotted arrivals, scurried
departures

My crafted pose of patience
upon every single one of your returns

Words crowd my head
I use them to sketch your slippery shifting shape
into a mediocre resemblance of the hero I deserve

What happened to us, to the people we used to be
our dreams became ash
what happened to the shimmer of our sweet eternity

Despair that wasn't there, disconnected from each other

I give free reign to all those words, still use them now and
again
recalling it all, when Barbie met Ken

Lips whisper forever at first brush
falling
 falling
  falling
it feels like love

Oohs and aahs at the ring winking on my left hand
a glass or two of bubbly to ease that jittery sensation

Radiant and smiling, gliding down the aisle on dad's arm
promises exchanged, another magical kiss, our charmed life
began

Yes, I let you in, allowed you to drive clean a stake
a heaven-sent thunderbolt
somewhere south of sweet and virtuous into all my
restless hungry places

Now nothing of you remains for me, to touch, taste or feel

Memories live on despite the death of dreams

I have none, nor will I request your photograph or carnival
bears
trace evidence of exchanged trinkets

Not a letter with your flourished signature
nor a soft patch of skin proclaiming your name
upon my body

There was a time when I did craft poems upon your bare
scented skin
with my soft sweet little girl's tongue

Worn down your tough-boy bravado
with nothing but whispered promises of more

Indeed, I acknowledge your fair warning
Pretty girl don't fall in love with me
I never shall
You have my word.

Winter 2022 by Jill Sharon Kimmelman

You Are the Poem

I will wait for you

You are the poem that fills my heart
this morning

I sip my coffee, your favorite dark brew
cinnamon-scented with vanilla, lots of cream
just the way I always made it for us

I selected your rooster mug with the tiny chip
from our shelf of mismatched mugs
you had bent down to place sweet kisses
upon my rosy lips when it slipped
from my grasp

Do you remember?

I keep myself warm bundled deep
within your sweaters
my spirit nourished from the pages
of your letters

You are the dream that I will awaken from
when I feel your kiss upon my cheek

Come home safe to me.

Summer 2009

Author's Note: This poem was gifted in 2009 to *Delaware Boots On The Ground*, a non-profit organization that assists all of Delaware's Military Members & their families using individual & corporate donations.

You Are The Poem was presented to each soldier upon deployment to the Middle East. In addition, this poem was posted on the *Messages From Home* section of their website to facilitate on going communication between our courageous troops & their loved ones
back home.

Concussion

I didn't choose to say
             yes or no
when a falling lamp knocked me
             to my knees
not a soul beside me on the floor
                         no one to hear my whispered please

Placed like a sausage inside a tube
incessant knocking
                 relentless pain
Good news!
    no stroke or bleeding brain

CONCUSSION

Rest your brain
    i'm trying

Rest your brain sweet child
        tears are a waste
                now stop that crying

Can you not see me
    can you not hear me
        I'm screaming inside

Someone tell me
    I'm not really dying

Rest your brain
    rest your brain
        can't you see how hard
                I'm trying?

Summer 2022 by Jill Kimmelman

Richard Fireman

We are Waiting

I am waiting to meet the son of my friend
who died a year ago.
I remember when I first met his father
fifty years ago when we were young.
I was his son's age then
and had dreams too.
We thought time would last forever.
It did not. It is here
for me but not for Bob, his father
who could never have imagined
he would not be here.
I go outside to look at the meteors
which are supposed to come out tonight.
I am a man waiting for the stars
but they do not appear
just memories and hopes
like we had, like we have always had,
all of us, Bob and his son and myself,
all of us waiting for the universe to catch up to our dreams.

Nest

bird alighting

on the cemetery stone

a peace to be found

with those I never knew

the future never turned out

as we expected

space imagined as the ultimate frontier

when time was young

now feeling further from space

and closer to time

I begin to understand

the purpose of the trees

Contact

I meet the eyes of the squirrel
in the tree that is his home,
his world. In mine I set my room
in order, sculpt debris
to shape the shell of my life
carving away the detritus
hoping for a pearl
shining like the sky I look at
out my window, out my tree
looking to catch God's eye
– will he smile or cast stones?
I am looking through the rain of words
through the tunnel in the sky
to land. Once I was in Kansas
hypnotized by tornadoes in the sky:
the creation of something out of nothing
that proves that something was there all along.

[previously published in Worksheets 67]

Angling

The kite-flyer does not move
but soars, kisses the air,
makes vicarious love to the sun.

He stands patiently at the edge of the sky
unreeling his unbound self,
sensing the shifts of the wind
like a blind lover,
and takes what shapes
emerge.

We are so far from God,
so near.

[previously published in Monmouth Review 45.2 SPRING
2002]

Not My Little Troubles

I who had never really believed in God
was left to comfort her with her belief.
Her two brothers were dying a thousand miles away
and all she could do was cry. I walked her to her car
and told her to believe God would take care of them.
She smiled and thanked me without knowing I had no idea
what I was saying, just thought it would serve best,
just didn't know what else to do. I did not make
the sign of the cross or star or crescent,
said no other words, just listened to the birds
that made no sound, looked at the sky and hoped
there was more there than I could see, some point
that would transform my ignorance and her pain,
some shape beyond the snowflakes' crystal.

Richard Fireman

New Worlds Need Names

This time it was all going well
but as we watched the TV
she said it's going too well,
something's going to happen.
At the end of the show I got ready to leave
and she asked me to take her home.

She was home. She didn't know
like she didn't know I came to see her each week
or what a galaxy was
or how to tear a tissue.
She couldn't understand how I knew she'd be there,
how I'd know what planet to point the ship at.

As I write this I hear on the news
we sent up a rocket to catch a piece of a comet.
On the way home on the radio is a story
of snow falling on the living and dead.
Outside the car freezing rain is falling.

Last week my mother said "Pop is coming"
but didn't know whose or the difference.
In the old days they were wise to make constellations
when they didn't know where they were heading,
to recognize what was too far away.

[previously published in <u>Writing Away the Demons,</u>
Northstar Press, May 15, 2009, Chapter 8: The Words that
Built a Fortress]

Take it, Leave it

I walk into tho rain. I let it
pour on me. It doesn't matter. Death
happens. Illness happens. Time
moves. It's the mood I'm in
since I talked with my friend, since
I asked him how he's doing and he said
lousy, I've got cancer. And it's spread.
A sign of the times that the second statement
was needed to really scare me, or him,
like a Hollywood sequel to a monster picture.
But the time is not advanced enough
to hold back all the tears, to ask
who he's told, who not, what
he's going to do, what can I do.
Or for him to tell me what a friend I've been
and that he loves me. Damn him
for making me remember I love him,
damn him for being human, damn
us all for running out of god damn time.

[previously published in Monmouth Review 47.1 FALL 2003]

Richard Fireman

Prufrock is starting to make sense

I am still a young man
                    no longer.

Half the music that makes me move
is by people dead or unremembered.

I've known my best friends longer than a generation.
What I believed in has come back into style.

"One new white hair for each new pain"
may be the best line I ever wrote.

I am haunted by my own words,
not immortal but still living
                    past their time.

Richard Fireman

Walk to the mailbox at night

Before I go back inside
I pray I will never not care
to look up at the stars
wink at the moon
say goodnight to God
until we meet again

Richard Fireman

No Way

No, there will never be the perfect poem

    and the sun will never keep from setting

No, there will never be the perfect life

    dream's leaves will always fall in autumn

No, there will never be the perfect love

    there are tornadoes even in the spring

No, there will never be the perfect death

    as summer's green becomes the white of
winter

[previously published in Monmouth Review 48.1 FALL 2004]

Rodney Richards

Charlie's Tree Service (*To my brother and his crew*)

seventy-foot-tall oak tree
looms majestic on neighbor's
front expanse. Charlie's men
appear to obliterate its
commanding presence

spurs on, ropes high, Chaz
climbs as his chainsaw
screams, buzzes through limbs, branches tumble as callused
hands below push and feed the piercing chipper's orange
grinding jaws

sunrays higher as only wide trunk stands upright, unencumbered
a ton of chips fill the truck. muscled men soaked with sweat
guide long spinning chains, slice sections in quarters
rake lawn and street debris into buckets overflowing

the pounded scrapped mini forklift loads heavy chunks
"clunk" onto trailer's bed as stump grinder hovers
over wide roots. rotating pressure shatters, chops the base,
earth lies dirty, flattened under wood bit mounds

proud of brother's abilities, Maggie's lawn
spotless, no signs of expended efforts.
his pro crew exceeded expert expectations

sit on my cherry bench across the street, shadows
of the oak's tall beauty now deceased
it no longer blocks sun's glare from the east.
birds will nevermore roost in its skyscraper branches

only photos, memories,
keep the mammoth shade tree alive, a canopy
of green-leafed space, a storm wind threat
smashing the split-level's roof

fated, it disappeared into living glory

Ellen's Underwear

finish warm shower, towel off vigorously
place left foot in, right, lift high to waist
your 95% black modal polyester clings
tight, a soft fuzzy sock slick as silk

your printed label *The Ellen DeGeneres Show*,
laughed aloud at her pranks and foolish games.
went online and bought a Christmas pair of
kelly green, yellow trees, red buttons aglow

every morning push Winston left out of habit,
millions of tv followers dress on both sides.
your mid-thigh cut calms and comforts torso
name on your label in Sharpie IDs you as mine

first saw you 20 years ago as watched commercials
bypassed wide loose-fitting Jockeys and Hanes since.
needing change, you didn't disappoint or fray,
wearing your pants Ellen, feels manlier every day

Kryptonite Green and Hard

hear Happy New Year! smiles on
a great new day, prosperous times ahead
implied. But you no longer by my side and
what future left—bleak and lonely—instead.
covid stung you before the vaccine could

you sniffled with flu which jumped swiftly
into your lungs like lightning striking a strong pine.
that tree was me too my love, until, unprepared
flashes of pain, remorse, ended decades intertwined.
helpmates to our cores, 1000 times more

drove to hospital but wouldn't let me enter
sat in my truck, prayed hard, *blasted winter*.
tears gushed when ventilator shoved in
could only imagine your body lying grave.
eyes dreamed of more days alive until older

they said you lasted thirty hours breathing,
fighting, the invasive invisible virus, but
microbes stronger than Superman's skin once
kryptonite snuck in. i cried with head in hands.
broken heart ripped apart until shredded

beg God's happier place for you now my love
gone from this place of suffering and travails.
will wait my turn to join you again, eternal
mansions and gardens as once we were in.
there, sacred, a palace where no kryptonite dwells

Oscar Night 2022

keep my family
  out yur fuckin' mouth
yelled Will to Chris in front of cameras.
  a billion tv screens rocked and swayed

audiences witnessed the slap in the face
  seen a minute before, shocked gasps
propelled Oscar ahead in the ratings race.
  most thought it staged for a thrill

how would i handle the same
  i wondered, if an ignorant comic
dissed my faithful loving companion.
  feelings blast atomic when least expect it

abuse me instead, i'll defend myself
  insult my mate though and receive
my uncoiled unchecked wrath.
  bomb ukraine however, and no one stops it

righteous outrage has passed
  punishment must fit the crime
take away the golden statue, guns, and toys.
  stop acting like little boys, act like heroes

Little Time Left

Two minutes to midnight...
Did not know it was so near
The seconds tick down to doom

Ten years ago it was six minutes to midnight...
We were alarmed when hands moved closer
Two minutes to midnight now

Wars in Syria, Yemen, and Israel grind on...
Peace is a chimera, a dream, we never achieve
The seconds tick down to doom

The mighty US of A sends ambassadors...
Brokered peace pacts hold for only days
Two minutes to midnight now

Afghanistan's war lasted twenty years...
Taliban fighters took control from ours
The seconds tick down to doom

Russia invades and bombs peace-loving Ukraine...
Citizens murdered, bombs lay buildings to waste
Less than two minutes to midnight now

Too soon, only 100 seconds to the end of life...
Eight billion wishes for more time quashed
With few heartbeats left, seconds tick down to doom

Shakespeare saved me

You have my love, yet I'd been so damn cruel,
sent sonnet forty as heart's hope was spurned
The bard's words of allegiance added fuel;
lit a spark for this devil overturned
Blame only myself for bruises I left,
once made they banished your sweet embraces
Your stony avoidance left me bereft,
as firm refusals meant no future missus.
Love knows it is a greater grief by far,
to bear love's wrong than hate's known injury—
Yet God's miracle nudged your heart ajar,
grateful, grace opened its locked safe for me
    Sorry is not enough and words can't state,
    we must be friends in love, not future's hate

Sonnet 40, sent in 1968 after altercation:

Take all my loves, my love, yea, take them all:
What hast thou then more than thou hadst before?
No love, my love, that thou mayst true love call—
All mine was thine before thou hadst this more.
Then if for my love thou my love receivest,
I cannot blame thee for my love thou usest;
But yet be blamed if thou this self deceivest
By wilful taste of what thyself refusest.
I do forgive thy robb'ry, gentle thief,
Although thou steal thee all my poverty;
And yet love knows it is a greater grief
To bear love's wrong than hate's known injury.
    Lascivious grace, in whom all ill well shows,
    Kill me with spites, yet we must not be foes.

Will stay married to Janet always

Rodney Richards

Why Don't I Ask?

what's wrong with asking *how was your day*
i hardly do, not nearly enough,
we'd both feel closer if i did

i'd have to listen to your answer,
open my heart, feel twinges of empathy,
care what your day was like, who you saw,
what children activities you helped with

my lips frozen; questions don't emerge.
my heart, buried under Himalayas, consumed
by Jeopardy answers, what you'll fix for supper

have always been blah, aloof, disdainful,
as if a king, all vassals bowing to my wishes.
worse to believe I'll survive without you near

yet we need each other or would be alone
     that drives me crazy

you long for my mind to hear you, body and lips to engage,
a heart to love your quirks, flaws, strengths, and stories

i do not want to die alone, you not near my bed, but will
unless give a hallmark card, flowers, boil a cup of tea,
or hug and cuddle without being asked

damn poor at building our relationship,
arrest and lock me in a cell for apathy.
it's the king you know
of seven deadly ways to murder marriage

Killing Time

killed an hour before dawn's light
    slaughtered it like all the others.
no hesitation or long opines
    it had to go like cherished brothers

milked two cigarettes to their nubs,
    drunk wawa and dunkin coffees too.
listened to car radio, checked iphone messages,
    killed off half from its drawn-out queue

sit here in front of my electronic typewriter,
    how long these words destined to last?
since printed on mortal diaphanous paper.
    these pages will crumble, not mark my past

killing time—as easy as ignoring seconds.
if I can shoot the bull,
    can shoot the clock.
whenever I doubt what action to take
    pull out a smoke, sip hot coffee,
    and grab my glock

Muse for a Poem

only takes an hour   to crank forth a poem
thirty minutes to draft
  thirty more—polish and craft

not enough days   to type what whirrs in my head
pop songs or breaking news on car radio
  inspire verses and words to be transcribed

a memory or observation   and free association
all fodder for poetic forms and gyres
  to manifest unforgettable sights

words appear verse-like in mind's eye   easy to convey
enjamb a line as intriguing
  as conversing with a stranger passing by

images inside poems   made of letter sounds
both a joy and clever fun to compose.
  to me, as lovely as Joyce Kilmer's tree

  it's okay, for now, they're just mediocre

Sick and Tired of Radio

Let It Be the Beatles
sang forlornly and John
*Imagine*d a world gone of
hostilities, *Free to Be… You and Me*

the Stones' *Street Fighting Man*
(Can't Get No) Satisfaction when
people like us with guns
Shot the Sheriff who's corrupt as hell

*We Didn't Start the Fire*s
but Cat's preoccupied with *Father and Son*
who are *Free Falling* with *Lucy* Arnaz
From The Sky With Neil *Diamonds*

Bowie's Major Tom is not alone in space
while sad Elton's *Candle in the Wind*
and the Loving Spoonful
Crash drumsticks with the Styx

We Are The World crooned Michael, as
the Motown sound sang choruses for Africa
after Detroit and Watts burned and
Holocaust remembers *Never Again, Never Again*

I watch, I listen, I whisper,
"Angie, ain't it good to want to *be alive…"*
yet I'm fed up with crude and bawdy DJs
and radio commercials that play again and again

at least new covers break up the ennui

Sue k Green

My Reality

Out my window,
an amazing sunrise,
an unforgiving world

Filled with challenges
touched by personal experience
colored in historical references

Flavored with religious beliefs
mired with weeds of crises,
shaded with deep roots of love

Filled with
       patriotic beliefs, equal rights, fair elections
       loud voices, alternate interpretations

Fraught with
       political division, prejudice
       fears of random violence
       war, death, destruction

My soul cries for homeless victims
My heart beats for tomorrow's promise

I search for truth
consider consequence,
follow my conscience

You and Me

Like an asteroid
you fell into my life
filled the black hole
of my existence

With strength of soul
you rocked me
with the rhythm
of your heart

Like a tidal wave, you
washed away my sorrow
helped me bloom
like a spring rose

When your expression of love
changed with the seasons,
began to smother me,
I had to leave

I was ready to plant my own garden
where my newfound seeds of ambition,
my own flowers of thought
had chance for real growth

5/14/2022

It Falls to Us

A Democracy perceived:

> *of the people*
> *by the people*
> *for the people*

> *with constitution, rule of law*
> *three branches of government*
> *individual and states' rights*

Our red, white, and blue
stars and stripes
on proud display

We have been blessed through the years
with patriots who have fought and died

Today we witness

> *a dysfunctional Congress*
> *a nation divided with cult-like reverence*
> *false rhetoric spread on mass media*
> *blatant disregard for law and order*
> *a violent attempt to overturn an election*

Our generation needs muster courage
    support honest leaders
    hold accountable those who seek to divide
    confront challenge from whence it comes
    restore, reform, rebuild, preserve
    for all future generations

1/9/2022

Singing in the Rain

Alone on the path,
no bird song in the heavy air
no squirrels in their usual scurry

I walked under a grey sky
in step with the musical beat
of a light April rain

Overhead, the sky grew darker
wind gusts threatened my pace
heavy rain drops fell like drumbeats

I quickened my steps toward home

5/14/2022
Singing in the Rain is a 1952 American musical comedy

Death's Call

Her last word
spoken
her last breath
taken

Her hand lay limp in mine

Was it real, or
did I only imagine
a shadow rise up
as her soul took flight

If the soul be the essence,
the energy, the spirit
of life itself
from whence does it come
and, upon death,
where will it travel?

Loved One Lost

In the light of morning dawn,
the moon lit sky at night,
tears fall as ocean tides
on sandy shores of grief

In most fragile tones, we cry out,
console each other, pray that peace
be found in the heavens

Still, we see
an empty seat at the table,
miss a loved one's presence there

2/7/2022

Night and Day

Another night fraught with
shadows from the past
scenes that disturb in all
too vivid nightmares

I awake to streams of sunlight
that filter through my window,
smile with hope and promise
on this new day

1/26/2022

Cost of War

An unprovoked war, a Russian invasion
rockets, bombs, tanks
civilian centers not spared
homes, hospitals, schools crumble

Casualties grow, bodies torn apart
lie amidst debris, line the streets
survivors search for other life
mass graves dot the horizon

Millions of refugees, mostly women and children
leave their homes, cross the border
Russian forces destroy rail lines
fire on negotiated humanitarian corridors

Men and boys stay to fight
strong-willed Ukrainian forces
struggle to save their families, their country
detain, kill, slow the aggressor

Their President speaks out,
refuses to leave the capitol city,
encourages the fight, pleas directly
to world leaders for help

The West stands unified
United States, NATO, European Union
send much needed supplies,
condemn, sanction the aggressor

Reporters risk their lives,
record the devastation
in horrific tones, inform the world

4/23/2022

Sue k Green

The Children

The schoolroom full
young faces smile
eager to learn

"Boom"
they fall to floor
hide under desks

Window glass splatters
walls fall, children
in, on, under rubble

Beneath dark smoke,
within burning embers
lay small lifeless bodies

Severely shaken, still in shock,
a young teacher climbs out from debris
searches for survivors

She finds one small girl
lifts her up, cries out
into the foul-smelling abyss

*"You cannot kill our will to survive,
our determination to live free.
The children are our future."*

5/20/2022

Sunrise

I revel at the amazing sunrise
outside my window
a gift of light, full of promise

Give thought to the world
      fraught with division,
      hateful rhetoric,
      discrimination,
      war and poverty

Pray
for a better tomorrow
a world, its people
in much better light

5/2/2022

TARA X

LOVE X1

Lose
One Moment
Voice
Everything

LOVE X2

Loosen up
Over here
Velvet crush
Ecstasy's near

LOVE X3

Let yourself
Overwhelm me
Vow
Everything is for me

LOVE X4

Lonely live
Only one
Virtual reality
Escape everyone

LOVE X5

Let loose
Own your aura
Venture forth
Entertain life; pulsate with its plethora

LOVE X6

Love letters
Overstating sentiments of the heart
Verbose titillations
Eloquently you're tearing me apart

LOVE X7

Lovely lit and   lonely
One more chance   to be my only
Veil your thoughts   you're not so holy
Enjoy my high   a little slowly

LOVE X8

Let me embrace you
Over and over again
Vindicate my all
Every moment be love

LOVE X9

Lend me your calm
Offer its peace
Validate its power
Eclipse all harm

LOVE X10

Lately I have thought of you
On point
Vintage times
Ever increasing circles

LOVE X11

Let go of the mayhem
Overshadow the chaos
Venture with glee
Experience the infinite; everything is
                    just you with me

William Waldorf

A pillow

rests on my bed,
beckons
as I lie down.
it will collapse
to support my
  sleep, but
    I rise surprised
  to realize
it swished flat.

Like love
must be fluffed
nurtured back
each day—yours
fills my heart.

Biker

I hear it pant
see its leather jacket,
no helmet.

A grey tail hangs
from old glory's
headband,

green light.

Leaves with a growl
to vanish
towards his
focal point,

on his
Ponce de León
machine.

Draw of love

There are moments lovers of all ages
relish their attention, yet feel caution
deep within their hearts since being smitten
with hope. What will be their future chances?

Unable to be apart—absences
pull like magnets with enormous tension.
Not to be included or feel certain
make most flinch and require fresh glances.

As they'll look in other's eyes to be sure
that their love's relationship will endure
no matter what obstacles encountered.
Together they'll never feel outnumbered.

With time the power of love grows greater
as lovers find comfort with each other

Friends recalled

A black fan oscillates heavy air
in the humid Vietnamese
restaurant. To balance
the hot air like the cuisine
whose brilliant aromatics of heat
sweetness, sourness, and fish sauce,
like war, leave memories

With the Viet Cong life was about
yin and yang, sweet and salt.
Hot or warm, fresh, or fermented
downed with warm Ba-mu'ro'i-Ba Beer.

Lost faces rush back, under
that sticky spotted fly strip,
to recall forgotten meals.
Buncha meatballs with noodle
salad always with fish sauce

Pho bo beef soup or Pho ga
chicken flavored served
with rice noodles basil mint
leaves, lime, and bean sprouts

In summer
she loved Goi Cuon. those
shrimp or pork Spring rolls,
with the cold
peanut dipping sauce

A tongue can never forget a good meal
or war sex

L'dor v'dor

from each generation
to the next; love will rush like flood rivers
into the hearts of those little pishers
that everyone knows as their grandchildren

whose presence attracts every emotion
from those living who use their ancestors
to looks for clues to claim these loud squeakers
they play pass the baby for inspection

none will reject this smiling cherub face
recipient of the family's embrace
to be stored until opportunity
to transfer is forced by a new baby

All ages stand over life's miracle
who is swaddled beneath love's ensemble

One

Alone on my own is my fate.
I have none to collaborate
with or hear laughter shared.
Seems strange to miss this emotion.
Sounds are gone as if they're stolen,
a fact for the unpaired

who live within past memories,
like when we ate some blueberries
whose sweet-tart taste lingered,
calling us for most of the day.
Now your spirit sings everyday
to a lonely songbird

who aches for disappeared music
to join, to hear his lost critic.
This all changed since you're gone.
There are no echoes in my life.
Quiet is like a dull kitchen knife
that won't cut clean when drawn.

impressions of starry, starry, night

Next to a cypress tree in Saint-Remy
Venus rests atop the tail of a cloud.
Swirls like whipped cream caress a cobalt sky
white zinc whorls light the church steeple below
in Vincent van Gogh's textured starry night.

Bright crescent moon to balance the night sky
all around like Divine inspiration
hypnotic views that beckon, gratify,
this painter's perceptions from his passion.

Charcoal sketches process new schools this night
strong impressions, appear on this canvas
frozen stars will be given amorous
raves when in one's sight.

Cypress placed as obelisks link life to death
all around Earth's star, like Joseph's vision

are galaxies that surround all actions
they'll gather as you admire to take your beath

of shared emotion will withhold your breath
surrounded by galaxies from his action

as all gather to admire and share starry night

are galaxies that surround the artist
who viewed this night's show from his only star

shocked to know all of this came from his brain
seen inside not through his windowpane

Reflections

In front of the mirror, she blocks my sight,
as she tightens the towel 'round her head
a spare sucks water droplets as they spread,
her soft skin glistens from the embers light.

Jiggled dimpled cheek next to my love bite
makes me grin, as I recall that beachhead
slithery, serpentine, soft, copperhead
wiry, quick till' it was embraced just right.

Forced to release my love, I devour her
naked beauty that's lost in lust's ardor,
such a slim waist accents her full figure
elusive, although I'm her seducer

Favors of love can be given freely,
but, be more prudent for eternity.

Afraid to ask

You sit so still, staring out the window
a handshaking, you're breathing so softly
erect, distant, watching so intently,
my love, often wondering where you go

knowing we could overcome any foe
I miss you, my heart longs for you fondly,
angrily craving your return, nightly
tucking you in safely with your pillow.
My vow is forever. Will you know me?
Timidly, I'm always afraid to ask,
when I'm in front which person will I see,
happy knowing face or your granite mask?

I once had a love that filled me with joy,
sickness took it away, left a decoy.

William Waldorf

Whistle Away Fear

It can be argued that fortitude will grow
inside the mind to help with rejection,
if your dreams are delayed learn this lesson
to release your tension open lips to blow

out a tune you heard from a piano.
While fate forces you to be a showman
those moistened lips will still have the option
to adjust and give fate a counterblow.

Then someone will notice you're not anxious,
this will make you stand out, perhaps famous
no longer to be part of the chorus.
But that whistler who waits for his progress.

This is your turn as you begin your dance
to hear your music finally advance.

Kiev

A crucifix swings
upside down
from a nail
a painted Jewish star
fades on the wall.
Slowly down the memorial board
shade hides the next name
while down halls
war's wind tolls
gone, choirs,
gone, teachers
gone, students
gone, laughter.

Biographies

Carol Johns, a retired high school teacher, taught 27 years in the Monmouth County Vocational District. She is the mother of two adult children and has one granddaughter.

New to writing, especially poetry, she also enjoys drawing, painting, gardening, traveling, and especially cooking.

She lives in Long Branch, NJ, with her daughter and four cats, three of whom are much loved.

Dona McCormack is a poet, writer, and mental health advocate, with fiction published in Saturday Evening Post and Tahoma Literary Review, among others, and poems published by Spillwords Press, and forthcoming in Fine Lines. She has a Master's in Arts, in English and Writing Fiction.

She spends her time managing her writing career and her disabilities, working her garden, enjoying wildlife, her home, and her family.

Dona's first collection, love bytes/Love Bites, is forthcoming in 2023. From this collection, enjoy "Lilacs," "Right in the Kisser," "Epitaphs," "I Am the Poem," A Little Fire," and "Aphorism #2". Connect with Dona on Instagram: www.instagram.com/itcomesdowntochance

William Waldorf - Bill's love affair with poetry began with strict forms like sonnets.

Currently, he is focused on poems from daily life.

He loves to show that history has not changed us.

His latest book, *Sonnets and More* explores various themes of love's relationships.

Richard Fireman, writing for over fifty years, has given readings at several libraries and Barnes & Noble. Over a hundred poems of his have been published, mostly in the Monmouth Review, as well as the International Journal of Poetry Therapy, Passager magazine, East Meets West and others.

In 2009, he contributed a chapter to the book Writing Away the Demons, thirteen writers' stories of how each of them used writing to deal with life crises.

A collection of his poetry, Constellations, is to be published by Prolific Pulse Press in December 2022.

Jill Sharon Kimmelman is a two-time Pushcart Prize-nominee in Poetry, 2017 and 2021, and Best of the Net 2018 nominee. Jill has contributed to many back covers and themed anthologies globally. Her debut collection, *You Are The Poem*, a unique, 3-themed, poetry art book, is available online everywhere.

Jill's passions include reading aloud, "cooking from the heart," dramatic & musical theatre, book discussions, and photography of food & flowers. She lives in Delaware, USA with her husband Tim Little, and is a proud mother to her son Jordan.

elliot m rubin is a retired entrepreneur who has written eight crime novels based on Brooklyn, N.Y., two Jewish books of humor, and thirty books of poetry. He is also popular on Instagram. He has been published in multiple anthologies.

His website is **www.CreativeFiction.net**

Rodney Richards had poems first published in 2016. He published his bipolar rollercoaster memoir *Coffee, Cigarettes, Death & Mania* in 2021.

Two hundred of his essays on Baha'i spiritual and philosophical themes are in Volumes 1 and 2 of *Solving the World's Titanic Struggles,* originally issued online at bahaiteachings.org.

Since 2012, he's led weekly creative writing critique classes, and founded ABLiA Media LLC to help writers edit and publish their works.

Visit Rod at rodneywriter on Facebook or on his website at https://rodneyrichards.info

Sue k Green uses her poetry to express emotions, share memories, and record elements of historical and personal significance. In "*From my Heart*" and "*Stroke of Pen and Strike of Stroke,*" she focuses on the challenges of a new caregiver. "*With Rhyme and Reason*" is graced with intent, inspiration, and historical turns.

Tara X

I don't know how to describe my poems. I just write
What I do know is that creativity is a sign of being alive

Being alive is a blessing that
lasts for only now
There is only now
The lesson is a reminder that
every day
 is a better day
Make the most of it
There is health in creativity

Tara Chadha - doctor, poetess, actress,
 daughter, sister, aunt,
friend and lover

Love Deeply X
TARA

Contact Us

Contact us by email through rubin.elliot@gmail.com

Please include your full name and how best to contact you. Email preferred.

Additional poems and other books by poets in this anthology are available from various outlets, notably Amazon.com.

Thanks for reading!

We would be grateful if you'd post a review on Amazon or another venue, of your feelings and thoughts on the content or issues brought up in these poems. Your show of interest or Likes make a difference. We appreciate all feedback—it helps us improve and provides inspiration.

You can also find us individually on FB, Insta and other social media.

Thanks for your support!

The Thursday Poets

PS And write your poems!

We hope to read them someday and share in your experiences. It is easy now to independently publish at next to zero cost or hybrid-publish for a few hundred dollars.

Thank you for your patronage and support of poets everywhere

www.ingramcontent.com/pod-product-compliance
Lightning Source LLC
Chambersburg PA
CBHW071824020426
42331CB00007B/1599